Her Codependent Challenges

By

Nicole Tatara

Dedication

I dedicated this book to Todd Hinkle. He is not only my boyfriend, but my strength, my reason, and my confidant. Without him I would not be where I am today, on the right path towards healing and peace. We respect our individual differences and find unity in our families and beliefs. He is truly my soul mate and is there for me through all situations good and bad.

Todd, thank you. I cannot express my love and gratitude to you enough.

Acknowledgements

I would like to acknowledge author Melody Beattie whom has written numerous books in codependency including two of her texts that have reached me on a personal level: **Codependent No More** and **The New Codependency**.

Words can not express my gratitude to Melody Beattie for the healing and inspirational words that have touched me and guided me along the way in my own experiences.

I would also like to thank Dr. McConnell (the *real* doctor and PhD) who has immensely helped me over the last few years. He has recommended reading the texts of Melody Beattie in which I have taken to heart. Knowledge is power and I am fortunate to have been influenced by these two individuals.

Chapter 1

A "Normal" relationship. Julia had no idea what this was. Everything was either splendid or dreadful, being full of enthusiasm or doubt. A bad day here and there is to be expected, but her negative experiences throughout the years surfaced from her efforts falling to the wayside. She was her own deal-breaker in her relationships.

She sat in the office. A makeshift house to a place of profession. Situated on the south side of the main route surrounded by nice restaurants, homes, apartments, and other make-shift houses, like the dentist office next door. Julia was sure that the dentist office was a cozy 3 - 4 bedroom house prior just as this building was. A small receptionist window with slightly tinted pink glass separated the former living room from the former kitchen.

Behind the desk sat a receptionist, April, if Julia had recalled correctly. He was in her late twenties. Black hair and donned a stylist pair of brown, white, and teal trimmed glasses. She was very pleasant and had given Julia the usual and customary paperwork – HIPAA forms, medical and past history, emergency contact info – all that kind of stuff.

Julia was grateful that the office took later appointments. It neared 5:30 pm, which accommodated her work schedule nicely. It was dark outside being late December and Christmas was right around the corner. Julia found the white Christmas lights around the large picture window to be classy and gave her the warm feeling that most people get that time of year.

She finished the paperwork and returned it to the pale pink tinted window. April was prepared, She took care of the clipboard effortlessly while scheduling an appointment and typing one handed to boot. Julia was nervous, but tried to hide her anxiety the best she could.

"Dr. McConnell will be with you shortly." April smiled happily and Julia returned to sit. She was the only one in the waiting room. A wood painted Nativity scene sat on the ledge if the bay window encompassed by the small white lights. A small, yet tasteful, waterfall with rocks sat on a table against a wall on the opposite side of the room.

Julia sat back down squarely in the middle of the maroon sofa. The mahogany coffee table in front of her had an array of magazines from left to right and top to bottom in perfect overlapping columns. She couldn't have done a better job of laying them out herself. Everything from Time to Today's Christian was in front of her. She was nervous and doubted even being there. She knew she wouldn't be reading anything much at this moment, but chose a Parenting magazine which was right in the middle. This seemed like a good choice to her.

She glanced down at her thumb and decided to stop picking at it. A bloody thumb in the Psychiatric office would scream OCD. She hoped she didn't have that also, but found comfort in the perfectly placed magazines.

Julia leafed though the magazine vainly. Page by page stopping briefly to look at a title or a picture, but she knew she had no concentration right now to read for thought. Her tension was growing and her mind raced. *What if the doctor says I'm crazy? Will I need meds? What will my family think. I can't tell*

them. She subconsciously started picking at her thumb, just lightly, nothing extreme to draw attention. No one ever noticed her do that. At least that's what she thought.

The "new patient" paperwork was turned in 15 minutes ago and still no doc. *Come on.* Her patience was dwindling quickly. The pleasantness of the soft rock radio station playing non-stop Christmas music was fading as was the nostalgic frost that was building up on the picture window. She could barely contain the train in her head. She'd flip through, then check her phone, flip, check, send a text, flip, reply to a text, flip, flip, flip. She seemed to have a frantic system going on in a poor attempt to pass the time.

A door from one of the prior bedrooms opened and a mid-forties couple emerged along with a robust older woman behind them.

"Thank you." The woman sobbed slightly with a handkerchief to her face. Indistinct chattering carried on for a few seconds and the man had checked-out with April and undoubtedly paid the copay. The older woman, a Psychologist of some sort, retreated back to the room and closed the door. L. Dearborn was the name on the door.

One shrink per room. Julia thought. The man opened the door for the woman, neither speaking, and each got into a separate vehicle.

Marriage counseling. Julia instinctively knew, she knew the second the couple emerged from the room. *At least they weren't yelling in there.* She thought, giving them Kudos and wondered if she had ever went to marriage counseling when she was married it would have been a fiasco. The cops would have needed to be put on standby, for his sake. *Save it*

for the doc. She thought. She kept thoughts close to the surface of her mind that she wanted to ask the Psychiatrist. She was grateful that she picked a licensed Psychiatrist, and not just a Psychologist or typical therapist/counselor. She wanted the best education and prayed it lead to the best advice.

Julia was deep in her routine and didn't ever hear another door open.

"Julia." Dr. McConnell emerged out of the small hallway and into the conjoining living room. She stood right up and grabbed her things. "Yes. Hello." She walked across the room and instinctively shook his outstretched hand.

"I'm Dr. McConnell. How are you?" He asked very plainly, but full of compassion. Julia felt better about going to a Christian therapy office, more compassion. She followed him to his office.

Chapter 2

The room was painted pale blue, but the flat paint looked darker due to the dim lamps. A decent sized bedroom it would have been. Julia was nervous and like a stereotypical Psychiatric office there was a couch, but also a comfy chair, a coffee table, and the chair for the doctor. Julia sat on the couch, not in the middle like on the waiting room couch, but up against the left arm of the couch. It was a brown and tan colored couch, nicely upholstered. While sitting and getting comfortable she noticed a large box of tissues on the table.

"Hope I don't need those." She nervously joked. Not expecting the doctor to answer.

"Well, some people do. Will you?" He commented after a pre-mediated pause and she was taken back. Instinctively Julia looked around the room. A very impressive bookshelf to the right of the room next to a window and Dr. McConnell's chair with him sitting in it next to a small table with notebooks, a planner, pens, cell phone, and small various accompanying office supplies.

"Do patients lie down on the couch?" She asked and simultaneously pointed downward. "Like on the movies?" She inquired.

He didn't look up, but nodded.
"Some people find it more comfortable."

"Huh…" She found it odd, and decided to wait for the doc to take the lead. She knew if she kept rambling that she

9

would only look just as unsure about her being there, which was the truth.

He prepared a notebook with small sprinty amounts of writing. She looked at him briefly sizing him up. He was in his mid 40's with dark short hair and matching colored moustache and beard. Granted, if he was 30 years older he would have looked like Freud himself, with less facial hair. She prayed he would be able to help her.

His degree's and credentials hung on the wall behind his chair. Dr. McConnell has finished his introductory writing just in time to meet Julia's anxieties peak.

How could I have put myself in this situation? She thought just before Dr. McConnell spoke.

"Have you ever been to a Psychiatric office before?" He started the conversation.

"No. How does this all work?" She asked with a certain amount of uncertainty.

He sat there looking intelligent and educated while she did the best she could to speak.

"I've had problems with all of my relationships. Also, I have a lot of stress at work. I've had family members that have been diagnosed with bi-polar and I'm afraid I may have it also."

He replied. "Why do you think that you may have it?"

"Because I get happy and mad and sad and ecstatic all in the same day." Julia tried her best not to ramble while explaining.

"Uh huh." Was all he said with his notebook in hand. It seemed as if he stared at her while she spoke. Julia was 99 percent sure that her face was somewhat red by now.

She continued with his undivided attention. "This has always gone on. Almost every relationship." She paused. "Well, maybe not the first one. My first boyfriend." *My first love.*

Dr. McConnell took advantage of the pause in conversation. He shifted slightly and spoke directly and plainly.
"The way this works. Is I look for 'rabbit holes' it's one issue that leads to another and another until we get to the root of the what is going on."

"Ok. That makes sense." She completely agreed.

"Tell me about your first boyfriend. What is his name?"

"Dave". Julia replied bluntly. She knew he would be an issue, a topic, a large rabbit hole in her life for years previous and years to come.

"Tell me about Dave."

Julia had closed her eyes.

Chapter 3

_____

Flashback No. 1

Opening her eyes meant an awakening. A simultaneous flooding of emotions. She remembered every detail, as she often always did. The sights and smells of that May afternoon walk was powerful. Huge swaying long branches of poplar trees standing like columns of a bright sunlit Saturday afternoon. Seventeen and in love when all was hopeful and budding and before the cynicalness of her mid-thirites kicked in. She was 15 years prior again.

Where she wished her life could have stayed. Hand-in-hand with her first love, Dave. Very few romances, especially young ones, last and Julia was completely sure their love would endure. And it did until that one blissful afternoon. They walked as they often did and then he spoke. Dave, his calm and handsome self, spoke those devastating words to Julia. It felt like a knife in her heart. He had broke up with her. Not for another girl or his freedom, but for his schedule. She really didn't care about all the explanatory words that he said all she could hear was the bottom line.

She wished it wasn't real. The whole thing a bad dream. Julia felt like she was in a black abyss of emotions. It was a slap in the face and it took all of her composure to hold back her tears. No rebuttal, no negotiating, she just stood there and took it.

Like any other teenager her world was destroyed, a life over. The last thing he said to her before she ran to her bedroom and cried was "We can still be friends." A common cliché' and a bad sign for any ended relationship often gives false hope. Julia didn't want to be 'just friends' he was hers and she was his. Until now. Alone. All she could do was cry, and cry, and cry until she fell asleep.

The momentary fast-paced reality of it all passed as if it was a black out. She felt pain, despair, and a pain in her heart. The last thing she remembered was her head in the pillow crying and screaming in her head.

"How do you feel you handled the break-up?" Dr. McConnell asked.

She had dabbed her eyes with the tissue from the perfectly positioned box and exhaled. "As well as I could have at the time."

"Do you wish you would have done anything differently? Said anything in that moment?" The doc's eyes were more compassionate and less textbook. "I wish he would have left it alone. I mean me. I wished he would have left me alone."

"Why is that? He didn't leave you alone?" Dr. McConnell's interest seemed to be peaked.

Julia explained how Dave kept coming in and out of her life. He would say he loved her and she'd let him come back into her life again and when she wasn't convenient enough or another woman caught his eye he was gone. This happened for years. It still happened, but as Julia matured in her more recent years she was able to effectively express her feelings and tell Dave to take a hike.

Dave was relentless.

Their turbulent history was sublime when they were together and self loathing when absent. Julia told the story well of their past, but carefully left out intimate details of the one February night when they were twenty, post super bowl party, they went too far and after tests and arguments the aftermath of consequence was that Dave had no interest in seeing his son, ever. The occasional bump-into-each-other at the grocery store with Dave's every changing wife and Julia's wonderful little boy left a lot to be desired. Occasionally a 'Hello' was exchanged, if their moods were mellow and not sour.

Julia had heard of the expression that Freud says there are 'There are no such thing as accidents.', but she liked to thing there was versus the painful sting of the occasional grocery store five second visitation session in the dairy isle.

She was beyond sniffling now and the tears flowed. Julia clutched to the tissue box like a lifeline and prayed that Dr. McConnell's following words would be the life line to pull her in.

He didn't speak. He wrote, not in his notebook, but on a separate piece of paper.

NO SELF PITY

NO SELF CONDEMINATION

She read the bold words that stood out and he explained the meaning behind them. Julia felt slightly better. Fear of expressing herself, blame, and guilt was always there.

The good doc explained that her emotions cycled and switched so fast, on a daily basis, that she was not bi-polar. She was codependent. This was just as bad to Julia there was no medication to take, no fast fixed. Lots of hard work. There would be more rabbit holes next week, more issues, more walls to tear down along with the tears.

Forty five minutes of the fifty minute session had passed. Julia felt hope and prayed that healing would be the end result. She had a meaning behind her actions and a diagnosis.

Julia was her own worst enemy.

"I can only help you if you want to help yourself. Here are some exercises I want you to do for next week and some suggested readings on codependency." He leaned forward and reached over the coffee table with the paper he had scribbled.

"Thank you." Julia shook his hand and exited the room towards April's window with guidance in hand. She scheduled every Tuesday night for the month of January and walked out

into the snowing and blowing weather, there was a winter storm evolving; she headed home.

Chapter 4

Julia read the first few chapters of the suggested reading, "Codependent No More." By Melody Beattie. Within the first five pages or so she was teary, shaking in the awakening of the reality of the words. The words described her to the hilt. She was stable yet flighty, happy yet sad, helpful yet resentful. The text went on and on.

"Oh my." A long sigh and a short sniffle. She flipped from page to page reading. Dr. McConnell had suggested the perfect book and there were another 2 books on the list. One was by the same author. Julia thought how of her character and her actions were impacting her life.

Originally when she sought psychiatric help she thought she was bi-polar. This was worse. Being codependent meant no meds that would help her; she had prematurely scared herself into thinking she was bi-polar. The good doc was right, she had to help herself. Julia's low self-esteem and quickness to anxiety have negatively aided her. She has aided others and felt nothing was reciprocated in return.

I need to love my self and put myself first. Julia thought and closed the book. Her brain was processing rapidly from her synapses lighting up. She set the book down on the end table next to the ceramic teal lamp with ivory lamp shade that she liked so much. Her living room color scheme was tan, teal, ivory, and black.

"Hi mom." Her son Charie strolled through the room from hallway to kitchen for the purpose of a snack. The twelve-year old boy of hers was almost as tall as her and had the attitude of an eighteen year old.

Loud clattering of leftovers held by plates and bowls were pushed and left idle in the fridge.

"Find anything good!" She shouted. "Think there are Hot Pockets in the freezer!" She paused and pulled on her left sneaker. "I'm headed to the library. Gonna take out some books. Do you want to come?"

"Nope mom. Headed to the mall with Steve and Mike soon."

"Ok." She nodding her head remembering and put on her right sneaker. *Everyday is a battle.* And she left the house.

Julia drove her SUV to the Brooks Library dropping off Charlie at the food court entrance. Her destination was a quick two blocks away except for the weekend traffic it may have been 5 miles away. It would have taken her fifteen minutes trying to make a left, but instead she took a right and drove a ways longer.

She went through a Starbucks drive through and an iced coffee was what she needed. A few blocks later she passed her ex-bf's house. Rather an apartment, or 'love shack' as someone commented once. She had mixed feelings passing by Ethan's. A high school acquaintance that was much more to her within the last few months, but not now.

Her anger and trust issues got in the way. She pulled him close and then pushed him away. That is when Julia sought

help. He could have been the one, but instead was another jaded ex in the path of destruction that she left.

Julia drove by. There was no car in the drive. Since the driveway was short she couldn't help but notice the absence of his navy blue Nissan. Ethan was her friend, lover, and confidant. She silently thanked him in her thoughts. She was grateful to him. Their relationship was short-lived and the end result was all worth it. She found help, which was the important thing, but it did not replace the cold empty nights.

The library was located on the shore of Lake Erie. Large boulderesque gray rocks matched the slate covered sky on that early January day. The turbulent spray of the water washed up and pulled back leaving the cold and wet water.

Julia noticed this while so much has escaped her. She walked and paused at the door. *Open 9 to 5.* She went in and Julia walked right past the Psychology and Philosophy section being quite happy with her self not dwelling on her current situation. She was doing something for herself. *Yes. Travel!* She was excited and Italian culture was her heritage. *This one…this one…* she perused the shelf and picked out a choice few. Books from Leonardo Da Vinci to traveling in the countryside filled her arms. She had lots of reading and research to do. Italy was a not just a place to travel to, but her heritage.

Someday I will get there.

Julia figured that if she started studying her Italian now she would be fluent when she travels abroad.

"Next!" Yelled the woman in her mid-fifties behind the checkout counter at the library. Julia walked up to the counter

placing five books down, all in sequence by size and relevance.

"Hi." Julia spoke and mirrored the good-natured woman's demeanor.

"Italy. Good choice." The assistant magnetically scanned each book. "It's snowing again and the waves look choppy."

"One snow storm ends and another starts." Julia was still in an exuberant mood despite the frigid conditions and charcoal-gray clouds waiting outside the automatic sliding glass doors.

Doing something good for myself.

Chapter 5

Mid February meant more snow with very few breaks in the clouds. Week after week of therapy helped Julia in small increments, but at times her life still felt unbearable.

"What am I doing?" was the text sent from Julia's cell to Susan's ipod.

"What normal people do. Date." Was the blunt reply. "Good luck! I want details later!" She wanted to encourage Julia as much as possible.

This was the last text Julia got from her bestie as she pulled into the Tim Horton's parking lot. She was happy the snow stopped, but the night sky was lighter and the air slightly warmer. Clouds and fronts were mixing.

She closed her car door with Charlie following as they crossed the parking lot. She instantly spotted Joseph and his son the moment they pulled in.

Joseph had stated the previous day. "You bring your kid, and I'll bring one of mine." It wouldn't be a very personable date, but at least she could see how he was with kids. If there was there with no kid, it was an instant deal breaker in her mind. She probably would have run him over while exiting the parking lot.

Joseph was very handsome. They greeted shortly in the lot, but immediately went inside to escape the cold. He held the door for her and her son.

Two hours later the kids were bored to death and acting up to get attention and kicked out. *Kids.* They both thought. Even though there was a 7 year age difference between the sons, they both wanted to leave. The mom and dad, respectively, did not.

He was nearly done with his extra large double-double coffee and she was half-way done with her medium café-mocha. With Valentine's day passing a few days before their first date they agreed to talk, chat, and text for a few weeks to get to know each other before meeting in person; the perils of online dating.

The restaurant was pleasant, being both their personal favorite. The best coffee, breakfast, and light lunch menu in town. Posters and advertisements of the company's junior ice hockey league hung on the walls as did left over white Christmas lights.

"I hope to open my own garage some day." Joseph was a mechanic by trade. He looked handsome in his gray and black Polo shirt. It went well with black metal rimmed glasses and dirty-blonde spiked hair, which was just the right height, the look suited him well.

His son, JJ, also made an impression. His light colored hair remained in a strip. Both sides of his head shaven, a Mohawk. *Cute, different.* She thought and sipped her coffee. Being liberal she thought this was encouraging while other patrons in the restaurants gave disapproving glances. Julia often let Charlie dress himself however he left. One day preppy

then to slobby, and her no-so-favorite mood – gothy, as she called it.

A mix of soft rock and country music played in the background. It was snowing again, but the warm glow inside dampened all of their surroundings. All the typical informative questions and responses were a short past away and talks of ambitions, hopes, and dreams flourished.

"I've always wanted to start my own business also, small of course. A retail bookstore." She smiled.

"We could always go into business together. A garage and bookstore. Customers can read while they get their vehicles worked on." He was serious and definitive in his spoken words."

Julia leaned forward, still smiling. "We could call it JavaLube. Java-coffee house and bookstore and Lube – the garage." Another half-hour of lighted conversation gave way to the end of the night.

"I love your red hair." He commented as he held the door open again exiting. He had admiringly stated this several times through the night. He was a sucker for red heads. *An Italian red head. It doesn't get much better than this.* He admitted to herself that he was smitten.

It was the perfect first date.

Chapter 6

Julia was fond of Borders. Living in a mid-size town meant limited choices of bookstores. She knew the store quite well and instinctively found herself in front of a towering bookshelf in between the Psychology and Self-Help sections. She knew the exact title, but kept her options open.

The limited number of meditation books, and specifically Zen and Mantra, would eventually be an area that she would frequent. But not this visit; this visit was vainly searching for another Melody Beattie work – The New Codependency. Julia had finished the first book, which was written a decade prior. She hoped this newer book would give additional knowledge and insight within the last ten years. To Julia it made sense. Obviously the great thinkers of early Psychology opened the door and many others since have contributed.

Contribute away. She thought while sliding the white and blue covered book out of its held place on the self. It was there, at almost perfect eye level, as if it was waiting for her. Behind her and off to her right was a dark brown leather chair that called to her. She sank right in effortlessly with her would-be bought book. Her momentary tunnel vision of text interpretation was suddenly, yet pleasantly, cut off. A stunning man with black hair with matching leather jacket moved uncomplicatedly from her peripheral to straight in front of her. *Also a Psych fan.*

He was quite easy on the eyes and as far as Julia was concerned the book might as well have been on the floor collecting dust. She didn't realize that she was staring. Subconsciously within a matter of minutes she could envision herself meeting, dating, marrying, and having a tragic end with this man. *Damn.* She felt foolish and stupid. It was the codependency. She knew this man and she would never exchange a full sentence within their brief fifteen minute shopping experience at Borders and yet the fantasy was there.

Recognizing this is half the battle. She got up and walked away just as he sat. The fact that she felt the way she did about it was the negative feelings that Dr. McConnell told her to avoid and not get caught into. She was like a computer in a constant cycle. Boot up, break down, shut off, log back in.

She still hated herself for it. "What am I doing?" She whispers to herself. *Why can't I get past this?*

Julia makes a selection of a Chicken Soup book, on sale of course, and is shocked beyond belief when she sees her ex-husband Ron. He was a few isles over in the cooking section with his new girlfriend. She didn't want to know her name or who she was; she just wanted to leave. The first seven years of Ron and Julia's marriage was mediocre and grew evermore bitter and by the tenth year when the divorce was finalized.

"Bastard." She said in a low tone. He never went to a bookstore with her and this woman had him whipped. She did not look familiar, but Ron always spent his nights with some other woman and showed no interest in Julia despite her lingerie and spiciness. *Obviously she made him come here.* Julia walked slowly towards the checkout counter near the front of the store. She had to pass the cooking section to get there. A sigh and long exhale as she walked, holding the small

stack of books. She wished she had chosen at least eight additional books for the sole purpose of hiding behind the stack to avoid seeing the couple. *At least they don't look happy.* Ron turned at an inopportune moment and saw Julia he flinched with jolting force and staggered back.

"Hello." She said plainly and took stock in that he was more surprised than she was. He could only reply in a rough "Hi" and tried to compose himself by latching onto the appropriately nameless girlfriend. Undoubtedly Ron did not want Julia to say anything to her or cause a scene. Within a moment she was standing tall and proud in the line up front of the store. "Woohoo". Another quiet comment. She knew he had a lot to stir about. Julia looked well that day, happy and composed in the situation; feeling a little guilty because of her gloating. Mr. Codependent Manifestation from the Psych section had taken the spot in line right behind her in line. With pairs of eyes following her, right or wrong, she introduced herself to Mr. Codependent Manifestation and took the opportunity to say "Hi."

It was very out of character for her, but it was very effective also as she caught a glimpse of the look on Ron's face.

Chapter 7

Three months had passed since Julia first started going to therapy. The snow was still present, but weakening in its daily intensity as March was in full swing. She sat on the same couch in the same office with the same doc and that same box of tissues sat there taunting Julia. She had needed them several times in her sessions, but not today. Today she was in rare form – hyper, excitable, and determined.

"You did feel the need to flirt with him in front of your ex?" he asked.

"Of course. It's been three years since I'd seen Ron and he wasn't very nice to me most of the time we were married. I feel that I have a small right to rub it in." Julia couldn't help but gloat.

"What are you rubbing in?" He was personally curious as to her response.

"Happiness." Though she knew that was far from the truth. Happiness came and went in medicinal dosage size cups, a few milliliters here and there.

The truth of it all Julia was never truly happy and had no idea how to achieve long-lasting happiness. Whether she was single, married, in a relationship or not, there was no way around her true feelings.

"How is it going with your boyfriend." He couldn't remember his name and looked for it written in his pages. She chimed in almost immediately.

"Joseph. He's fine. We are doing okay, I guess."

The good doc was not convinced. He waited for her to continue. Rabbit holes.

Julia's pleasure was replaced with somber eyes and a slight decrease in posture. "I get angry a lot still. Mostly after work. We've been dating for a few months and he still talks to all of his ex-girlfriends. Not just the ex-wife that he had the kids with, but other ex's."

"I see." Followed by lots of notebook scribbling. "Possibly the stress from work and the strain from him communicating with his ex's are leading to anger issues." He was confident this rabbit hole lead no where good. She nodded in agreeance.

He went on to explain. "All relationships are based on compromise. If he's not ready to give up talking to his ex's - what is he getting out of it. There is always a reciprocal relationship, give-and-take if you will."

This made sense to Julia. Why was he still talking to them? Not just one or two, but he was in contact with at least five or maybe more. Julia had never dated a man who has had so many ex-girlfriends and partners. She did not approve of his past and often questioned herself why she was with him.

"You know trust has always been a big part of my failed relationships. I try to trust, but it often seems impossible. I've gone through his phone, Facebook, and email. Every time

I do I find some conversation with some woman or ex that I do not like." She was hanging her head now. "I just can't trust."

"Yes. This is definitely a problem. Trust is a large part of any relationship. If you are not trusting of him, and now he is not trusting of you the chance's of this relationship working is minimal." Again Julia had thought *I am my own worst enemy*.

He shifted gears. "Have you found any useful tips in the suggested readings?"

"Love myself." It was not really a response, but more like an omission. *I need to love myself and put myself first more.* Julia slowly over the last few months of therapy and readings had come to the conclusion that several situations and experiences have contributed to her codependency.

First, there was her self-esteem. She often thought if she put herself aside it would be better to deal with any difficult task that would arise in her life. Second, her son had behavioral problems and therapists were needed when he was younger. Third, volunteering for several years in the medical field. Julia continually gave and gave until she was drained.

Love myself.

"If you and Joseph wanted to come in together we can do that." He threw the offer out there to her. Dr. McConnell wanted her to have a normal relationship. She wanted the same thing, at least for once in her life.

Chapter 8

The knob turned to their apartment door. Joseph took merely three steps inside and Julia was waiting in the kitchen. She had scrubbed every dish, rather forcefully, the kitchen table, and the counter. The damn room was nearly spotless. Every bit of bacteria scrubbed away by her anxiety.

"Are you cheating on me!" Julia yells at him in tears and enters living room. Joseph had kicked off his Nike's and they landed haphazardly on the maroon carpet, as they always did. This typically would make Julia sigh, but today, now in this moment she was in rare form.

"No." He was taken back from he accusation and her hostility. "Why you asking me this?"

I know he's lying, I know it.

All at the same time Julia felt anxiety, fear, anger, and jealousness. "I went through your text messages!"

"You did what!" Now he was mad.

"Yeah. Checked your phone again. It's bad enough that I have to put up with Lisa and now you are talking to all these other bitches! Every time I get suspicious I always find something!"

"They aren't bitches." He firmly corrected her.

"Ok. Hoes." Bluntly stating with her hand on her hip. She knew she was better than them and if he knew it too and loved her then Joe wouldn't talk to them often.

"Not Hoes. They are nice people." He was calmer, but she was still fired up. The adrenaline fed the fire and she didn't want to put it out. "The one we saw while shopping looked like a prostitute. She had fish net stockings and a mini skirt. I'm sure she's a really nice person and I'm so glad that you two text each other and send Facebook messages almost every day."

Julia knew she was right. *I am right.*

He couldn't have it all. He can't act like he's single and be in a serious relationship. Julia vaguely remembered what the doctor had said, but she did not want to follow it.

"We usually talk about the kids and how they are doing." He seemed sincere in his words and demeanor.

"None of that is in the conversations." Granted there was nothing sexual in the texts, but comments that can be taken the wrong way. Julia did not get inside jokes and took phrases like 'I miss you.' to be an act of betrayal.

"Well good. Why don't you break up with me then!" He was now shouting. "I've broken up with other women for less. Can't believe you went through my phone!" He mimicked her at first and then chose to ignore her. He thought the whole thing was ridiculous. Joseph plopped down on their couch and turned on the tv. He had continued his game of Fallout NV on XBOX 360 while she stomped and spat about. He chose not to listen anymore.

They kids all retreated to their rooms to play. They one thing they knew was that when grown ups argued to stay in their rooms. In all fairness it was their first big fight, but in their lack of responsibility they should not have moved in together only after a few months of dating.

More mumbling and slamming of drawers echoes through the kitchen. Joseph heard the occasional word, but he kept quiet and wanted to keep the peace he lost focus on the background noise except for the infrequent "ass" or "bitch" word that come from the kitchen.

"Die bitch! Die!" He yelled.

She flew in the room as fast as a hawk stalking it's prey. "What did you say!" She yelled in response half leaning into the living room.

He had no idea she was standing four feet away yelling again. She looked at him angrily, turned her head and looked at the tv. She gave a huff and returned to kitchen; she was irritated about being ignored.

Joseph had put the game on pause. He got a glass of water and mistakenly left a remote control on the kitchen table; the table that she just cleaned. He had just exited the bathroom to return to the couch and the black blur flew past him and landed on the loveseat on the apposing wall. The successful hurdle which got his attention. *He's not going to ignore me now.*

"What the hell!" He yelled; growing more irritated.

"You are not going to ignore me! If I wanted to hit you I would have." She was still angry and barely remembered

why. The voice of reason and professional guidance that she had sought fell to the wayside. It's as if she fell off the wagon. Julia's wagon was an emotional one.

If Julia knew one thing it was how to hurt people. She was good at it, but did not take in excellence. She wanted him out of the apartment. No necessarily permanently, but for now he had to leave. She knew him better than anyone, but she did the unforgivable. She insulted his kids. After a few "FU's" and a slammed front door Joseph and the kids left.

The guilt immediately followed. The following day she would schedule another appointment with Dr. McConnell.

Chapter 9

I'm back. The blue-patterned tissue box was replaced with a light green flower patterned box. Still right in the middle of the table. *Wonderful.*

"What happened after the fight?" He asked.

She was afraid that he was judging her. Julia felt ashamed that she lost control, the guilt aftermath. Which was also the enemy. "After Joe and the kids left then I sat in the bathroom and cried for a while.

A nod followed by note taking.

"Once I felt better I laid down for a while." She picked her thumb slightly from her nervousness.

A loud clap of thunder came from the storm outside. Spring brought mixed hot and cold fronts which results in the dark clouds and flashes of light in the sky. The spring day started near sixty degrees and closing twenty degrees less.

"Codependency is a vicious cycle. It repeats destroying yourself and the lives of your intimate partners. How did you felt like when you woke up after the fight?"

"Better. I felt better, but very tired." She admitted.

"Did they come home that night?" Rabbit holes.

"Yes. Joe only. He came home later that night. He dropped the kids off at their mom's house and then he went over his dad's for a while." She had stopped picking at her thumb and remained distracted by the intermittence of thunder and the constant rain.

"Did the two you talk when he returned?" He asked.

"A little. We talked about our relationship." She shifted her weight on the couch and straightened her posture. "I love him, but I don't feel that our relationship is fair to me." She was venting now and went on about finances, household work, and her feelings of always being second.

"I understand what you are saying." He added when Julia had completed her explanation. "Relationships are reciprocal and require lots of work."

She asked puzzled. "Why do I have to work harder? It always seems that I work harder and the men in my relationship never do."

Don't whine Julia you will get through this.

In truth, she not only at the deepest level wanted to have a successful relationship, but also a fair one. For once, a fair one to her. Julia's failed relationships were ever so troublesome to her. She didn't want to be alone, but half the time didn't want to be in a relationship either. Somewhere along the way she lost her happiness in couplehood. It always starts out great, but once it got to serious then she routinely became more serious.

I just want to be happy.

She began to cry.

"Why are you crying?" Dr. McConnell asked.

"I just want to be happy. I feel like half the time I am happy and half the time I'm not." Was her flat reply.

The doctor now leaned back in his chair more interested in what she was saying and scribbled fiercely. He was planning what to say next to Julia. He thought she looked nervous and she was. She was always nervous in his office and in general.

"Since you switch frequently from happy to sad have you identified your stressors, triggers, that seem to change your mood?"

"Yes". She nodded. "Sometimes his kids stress me out and my mood changes, but not all the time. Just sometimes."

She pointed to the rabbit holes and he explored them. "Does anything specific happen with the kids? What have you noticed that triggers your mood?"

Admittedly it didn't take much thought from Julia to tell her doctor exactly what was wrong. As much as she liked Joe's kids they also got under her skin sometimes as well. "They are loud and messy. When all three of them get home they throw their coats, shoes, and book bags all over the place. His son barely says hello and he runs to play XBOX immediately. His daughter doesn't stop talking and follows me constantly. Don't get me wrong they are great most of the time, but since they are younger then my son and I know that kids are kids. I guess that Charlie and I are more quiet and keep to ourselves more."

"Do you want to be in this relationship?" He asked.

"Yes." She was positive and assertive.

"Then keep trying. Work and prayer." He moved his hands when he talked. "Keep reading if you want to. There are other authors on codependency and self-help exercises that you can do. You will succeed if you try and believe that you can do it. At times it will be hard, don't give up. De-stress and take a nap if needed. Whatever you can do to break the cycle will help."

She thanked him again for the advice and exited his office out to the waiting room. Julia patiently waited for April to get off the phone to collect her insurance copay. She looked around the waiting room noticing the maroon and plaid themed décor. Quite the contrast from the Christmas décor from her very first session gave her a heart-felt comfort from the room. She left in the rembrandt drizzle of that passing spring storm thankful for the encouraging words and support.

Chapter 10

Flashback No. 2

She walked up the driveway with her heart in her stomach. She had to tell them, whether it was now or later she had to.

It will be ok. They will understand.

She carried the thick purple rectangular glass dish containing biscuits in one half of the divider and steamed vegetables in the other half. Dinner at her parent's house was going to be a good thing. Until she drops the news. A series of knocks and the door was unlocked and opened almost immediately.

"Hi!" Her mom excitedly screamed and pulled the dish from Julia's hands. "Common' in."

Everyone was there. A typical Sunday dinner with mom, dad, her brother and the dog. The aromatic smell of the beef tip casserole was overwhelming. Yum. My favorite.

"Hey." Her brother acknowledged her walking through the kitchen and snagging a biscuit. "Hows work?" He asks with a piece of it hanging in the right corner of his lip.

Nodding I answer. "It's great." And left that at that for now.

"Cool. How's school?" She was not ready to get into the subject of school too much. "It's good also." She half lied.

"Awesome." He sucked the remaining piece of biscuit into his mouth and made quick work of it just before exiting the room.

"I love how you and dad are redecorating the kitchen." Julia was quite content to be in the house she grew up in with her family. She had been in her own apartment for a few months. Her and her mom stood in the kitchen setting the table and finished the remaining of the prep for dinner.

"Damn!! Oh come on!!" was heard from the central location of the living room and echoed outwards like a microburst throughout the house.

"Dad's team must be loosing again." Julia said. It was usually her team that lost.

"At least it's not football season." Her mother replied.

Thank God for that. Was all she could think of in that moment. She poked her head in the living room. "Hi dad!" She had to yell due to the volume on the tv and glanced at the score.

"Hi Jules….Shit!" Was the reply from the recliner.

"Yanks are down four to one." She informed her mom of the score. Not that her mom cared much for the score, just how much a potential loss would affect dinner and the general

mood of her husband for the next few hours. In truth, Julia's mom was more concerned with herself doing her wifely duties like the cooking and cleaning and not necessarily the people who occupied the house.

Julia never thought that her and her family had a distant relationship. It all seemed normal to her. Normal is a difference of opinion.

Her mom stood over the sink and looked outside. Since it was spring she was happy that it did not rain today. "It's a lovely May day."

"Yes it is." She placed the rest of the silverware on the napkins and walked to the counter to get the ice and pour the drinks. A few finishing touches away and they would be ready to eat. Julia noticed her mother redoing the silverware placement. She vainly straightened each piece even though Julia had taken extra care in making sure they were placed perfectly.

This was her mother, nothing was right. Even at the age of twenty her mom still redid everything she did in the house. Dishes, cleaning, placement of pillows on couches, and vacuuming were just a few of the things that her mother did over and over tracing Julia's footsteps.

Julia held her tongue and tried not to make a face or show her frustration in her mother's actions. It's a fork. How perfect does it have to be?

Julia walked past the table and her mother. "I'm going to tell them that dinner is ready." She didn't ask her mom, she just went and heard mumbling behind her from the kitchen. She

tried not to care, she wished so hard that she wouldn't care, but she did.

Dinner was uneventful, and always the same. Mom mostly talked and her brother sometimes. Dad mostly ate silently and obsessed about his team losing. Julia asked the usual questions. How's work, how's the cabin, how's the garden coming along. Depending on the season there was some variation. Answers from the males in the house were one word or a small phrase occasionally. Good, fine, ok. These were among the most common.

It's almost impossible to have a conversation here.

Dinner was nearly over and dessert looked ok, but not desirable enough to make everyone stay at the table.

Here is goes...

"Work is going really good." She informed the table. "I was offered full-time so I'm going to take it." No one was affected. Yet.

"School isn't going that good, so...I'm not going back next semester." There it was. She said it. Everyone stopped eating, especially her dad with fork poised half way to his mouth. He had set it down somewhat forcefully.

"What do you mean you aren't going back?" The accusing question of clarification that she knew was coming.

"Yes. I don't really like it at the university and don't even know what I want to major in. I like what I'm doing now at the nursing home." She loved being a respiratory assistant and found the job full-filling.

Her mom was upset. *"What about insurance? When do you get insurance?"*

Julia didn't expect that question, but it was a fair one. *"Ninety days. Most probationary periods are ninety days."* Julia answered honestly and felt side swiped by the line of questioning.

"School is more important." Her father said disappointedly.

Her mother bitched. *"You would have been the first and only family member to graduated college in the family. What will your grandmother think!"*

Julia was taken back, but didn't say much. They were never permitted to say what they felt if it wasn't what her parents wanted to hear. Her brother kept silent; he was happy the conversation had nothing to do with him. Being four years younger than her he just turned sixteen and barely had a care in the world.

It went on for ten minutes and not a one of them asked her how she felt about it or if the decision would make her happy and be best for her. She wanted to finish college someday, but right now was not the right time.

Julia had always exceeded her parent's expectations in school and they expected perfection all the time. She was twenty and had a full-time good paying job, a reliable vehicle, and her own apartment. She felt hurt and everyone left the table and the kitchen, except for her. Sitting there still wondering what happened.

She left on that sunny May day walked down the driveway upset, mad at hell for letting her family treat her like that. She held back her tears until she drove off. She held back her tears, in front of her family. She always had to.

Chapter 11

"How did your parents make you feel?" Dr. McConnell asked.

"Awful." She balled and gripped several tissues in her hand. The green floral box was now on her lap. After several minutes of trying to calm down she was able to breathe and speak.

"Nothing I do is ever good enough for them. This was just one family dinner." She was now picking at both thumbs, hands flying as she talked rapidly with tissues in hand. The doctor listened and watched her mannerisms as she spewed. This was good. She needed to vent. At least she wasn't being passive.

"You are getting expressing your emotions; that is very good." The doc approved, but she did not feel like celebrating the ongoing break through that she was having.

He had analyzed that moment in her life. It was an important event in that her parent's disappointment and failure for Julia (and the whole family) to healthy express their emotions to each other. This conversation had negatively affected Julia for the last fifteen years. It was only second to when Julia had told her parents that she was pregnant. Also, a negative conversation.

Dr. McConnell was piecing together the rabbit holes and channels of her psyche, which was being paved, one step at a time. Julia's self-actualization was underway. Small steps being as they may have kept Julia on the path to healing. Setbacks were almost unavoidable for her.

"What do I do when my mind starts racing and I feel like I can't shut it off?" Julia was almost certain that she had asked this question before. It was the reassurance she needed; a validation that things will happen and it will be ok. Of course, the good doctor did not pacify or advocate any codependent behavior. He only acknowledged the presence of it.

"You should Journal if you can." He went on to explain. "Write down how you feel and what had happened to make you feel like that.

"Ok." Was her reply. Would she ever really Journal? Yes. Would she ever share it with the doctor? She was not sure of it. All the exercises he had given to her she had to read aloud in their sessions. Julia was never happy about this, but did it.

Julia's mind wandered while Dr. McConnell spoke about the healing power of prayer. She knew this. She felt she had a close relationship with God and didn't want to be preached at. He did no preaching, but she had difficulty being told what to do.

"I do pray, everyday." She reassured him. Julia was interested in the heart of the matter.

My heart is in the right place.

"What do you do to relax?" He inquired.

"Several things. I like to read, play tennis, once in a while play video games with the kids." He gave a puzzled look.

"Does playing video games with the kids really help you relax?" He knew the answer,

"No. It's not really relaxing, but it's something I enjoy." She said plainly.

A fair response he thought.

"I've been trying different types of meditation." She added.

"Good." He liked that response. Something to build on. "Tell me more. What kind of meditation?"

"I first tried Zen. I found it to be relaxing. It's easy to get lost in thought and I like being at peace with myself and the universe." She was happy with the meditation choices that she made.

Dr. McConnell scribbled in the notebook. "Is there anything you do not like about Zen?"

"Yes. If I do it when I'm tired I will fall asleep."

He gave a slight laugh and smile followed by more scribbling. Julia was sure by the time he was done treating her he would have wrote an entire book. – scribble, scribble, scribble.

Her mind drifted again and wondered if that beautiful rainbow was still outside following the afternoon rain. It was a

full rainbow, which was rare to see. The tiny remaining rain droplets shown every color in the visible light spectrum so vividly. It stretched from west to east as far as her eyes could see and she felt lucky and humble to witness this. The rain, only temporarily, had moved on.

"After months of therapy how do you feel overall?" He asked.

Julia didn't like looking directly at him when she talked. She was so self-conscious. "Overall. The same as when I first started coming here." She was honest and simplistic in her answer.

"Do you ever feel depressed?" Another direct question. He was full of them, which she appreciated.

"Sometimes…I mean I don't sit around crying or anything like that, but I do feel that sometimes there isn't any more in the future for me. Even though I have a good life I feel like I will never achieve anything."

After a nod she noticed the absence of scribbling. "You don't feel fulfilled." He went on to clarify. "You have a good job, but it's stressful. You have a intimate relationship, but there are stressors involved from Joe's ex-wife and the kids. You have a hobbies, but they aren't enough."

She pondered this and agreed with him. The stress from the ex-wife would give anyone reason enough to be angry. Especially since Joe has not set up any boundaries and she has free reign over Julia and her life.

As they talked over each aspect of stress and what makes her angry she realized more that it was not all in her

47

head. She had real reasons to be angry and not a pre-conceived anger issue which Julia worried about for very little reason.

"You need to either remove the stressors from your environment or change the way you react to it." He added.

Easier said than done. She thought.

Her therapist recommended a low dose SSRI, an anti-depressant. She was not surprised. She had thought for some time that she needed additional help. Julia gratefully accepted the script. *Prozac 10mg capsule. 1 QD.* "If you do well on this we will gradually take you off if it in six months. It will help the serotonin levels in the brain; bring them down to a normal level. It will make those explosions of anxiety smaller and easier to deal with."

She was bound and determined to overcome this.

"Ok. We are done for today. When you go out to the front desk Julia make sure you schedule an appointment for next week."

She gratefully acknowledged his request. Julia could not help but to notice the date on her iphone while standing at the receptionist desk scheduling her next appointment with April.

I can't believe next week is May already.

Chapter 12

Julia sat on the floor of her newly decorated bedroom. She went with Earth tones and a Chinese theme to accompany her meditation. She felt the tans, white, black, and natural green tones reflected the calmness of nature. She sat on a black square comfortable pillow and closed her eyes during Mantra.

"Ohhmmmmmm....." She elongated the sound. It's the most basic of Mantra's. Being one with the universe was ideal in connecting with her surroundings and letting go stress.

Her dim lamp with black and gray shade cast only a minuet amount of light in the room. Her pictures of the Chinese symbols for *Peace* and *Happiness* hung on the cream-colored wall. The black fluffy comforter lay evenly over her queen-sized bed. With moss colored accent pillows. "Ohhhhmmmmm...." She tried to make the sound come from deep within her body and released during the exhales. Releasing the air and sound all while liberating the soul.

After a good amount of time; she estimated fifteen to twenty minutes may have went by before ending her meditation. Of course, when you achieve inner peace, even briefly, you loose track of time. She often did this is Zen, once she achived her Mu, inner peace was imminent.

After so many days she had came home from work angry she needed to find the right outlet for all the anger.

Flashback No. 3

"God damn it." I muttered to myself, yet it was audible enough for people close enough to hear. I already forgot what time the numbers read on the time clock when I punched out. I was halfway down the sidewalk enroute to the employee parking lot on the south side of the building.

I loved the sunshine and thought the large white fluffy billowing clouds in the visible area where both beautiful and looming. Though mid-may brought unseasonable warm temps in the 80's this spring she didn't care.

I'm so angry! I feel like screaming, but won't. I passed the other employees vehicles and made a bee line to mine. The quickest way from Point A to Point B is a straight line.

The previous experience was not pleasant to say the least. The vision of her boss cradling her head and yelling "This is bad!" was enough to make Julia furious. Once the shock passed then there was only anger. Anger. Anger. Anger.

"I didn't even do anything wrong." She softly spoke to herself. No one was near her now as she was near the rear of the parking lot. She thought how if Joe was there he would call her a "Debbie Downer" or some other meaningless name.

"Just great." She complained more under her breath. "I can't believe she acted like that and embarrassed me in front of all my co-workers like that."

In truth, Julia did nothing wrong. Between other employees in other departments messing things up and the fact that the law is the law she was compliant and ethical in her work and could not help the fact that no one else was.

Where are my keys? I fished them out of the purse and hit the unlock *button. After lobbing my purse and purple lunch bag in the front passenger seat I get in and slam the door as hard as I could.*

"Bitch!" And that was that. I was angry as hell and there was no changing it and no going back. Unfortunately, I always bring my work home with me and tonight was not an exception. My bad mood carried over into the evening and Joe and the kids had to suffer for it.

She didn't care how glorious the day was, she didn't care that her vehicle peeled out of the parking lot, she didn't care about anything at that point.

Anger was absolute.

She sighed and outstretched he arms gracefully. She reached and stretched and finished her meditation with some neck rolls. The memory of her pre-meditation days always gave her shame. She tried so hard to remember Dr. McConnell's words and used the power of positive thinking. In her moment of anger, just prior to starting her medication

treatment she was proud of herself for not outwardly exploding. It was the implosion that was just as worrisome.

Now, it was off to the gym. Kind of a backwards idea to relax first and then exercise, but then again she was an odd person. It worked for her. *Doing something good for myself.*

Chapter 13

Julia had always been slightly over weight, but since the birth of her son and with all the complications it was not a surprise that she had gained weight. Losing the weight wasn't really difficult – eating right and exercise. The hard part was she never stuck with it.

This will be the time. This is my moment. Julia was an optimist. Being codependent knew she would do great for a few weeks. Then something will happen and she will lose hope in all things in her life. The excuses will come following the absence of exercise. Then a few weeks later after gaining all the weight back she will start back with her fitness routine and healthier eating.

The codependent cycle.

It never ends.

Oh well. She thought. She walked in feeling proud of herself. She scanned her ID tag to get into the fitness club.

"Hi." She said to the attractive light-haired well-chiseled man behind the counter. The employee returned the greeting. After a quick change in the women's dressing room she headed out to the main area of the club. She selected her treadmill in front of the television playing How I Met Your Mother. *I love this show.* She routinely pressed the buttons and fell into her workout with ease.

After a quick half hour she moved to the second row of stationary bikes. A brown-haired, brown eyed man took a seat on a bike in the front row and two spots. He was quite the looker. Julia guessed he was close to her age. He was fit and she immediately started thinking of this man.

Julia caught herself staring and pretended to look at the television in front of him on the wall. She doubted that anyone was really paying attention, but you never know. Some people where creepers and watched other people – for no reason. She realized that she wasn't any better staring at the man wearing a navy blue Penn-State t-shirt and black and gray workout shorts. He pedaled faster than her, but he made her heart race more. She imagined if she was a thinner and taller that he would definitely be interested in her.

Just another fantasy. She shook her head to rid her head of the thought. Julia picked up her ipod and changed the song. The Edge of Glory by Lady Gaga. *Next song. Good choice.*

She concentrated on the tv, ipod, and anything else that randomly entered her mind instead of giving into her codependence. Before the end of the work-out and her retreat to the showers she had completely forgot about Mr. Perfect Penn-State and completed her fifteenth mile on the bike. She was bound and determined that she would succeed.

Success meant something different depending on the mood. Sometimes Julia felt thankful in the small moments in life and success in realizing how lucky she was to have what she had and the people in her life. At other times, no matter what personal and professional goals she achieved she never felt ahead, never felt good enough and there was always more to learn and more to do.

Today, she decided to weigh herself. *Down one pound.* She breathed in deeply and let the breath out slow. *Baby steps.* She told herself. If she gave in to disappointment that would be all it would take to get depressed. The month prior she had lost five pounds with out exercising and without dieting. Prior to that she worked out five days a week and ate all salads and fruit and gained two pounds. It was frustrating. Each time she felt down she wanted to quit.

This time was no exception.

Next week will be better. A crisis avoided with the power of positive thinking.

One small success at a time.

Chapter 14

Julia and Dr. McConnell's session was nearly over. They had discussed what she was doing for herself that was positive and how she was dealing with the various 'stressors' in her life. The stress was manageable with the help of medication and meditation, her weight was stable and slightly losing from her hard work at the gym and making good choices, the personal enrichment was through the roof thanks to the Italian lessons.

Then there was her relationship with Joe, the most important relationship that was effected by her codependency. The issues with her parents were not completely resolved or absent, but manageable.

"Joe is ok, just as I am." She hesitated and scrounged for the correct words. "He recognizes my issues and does his best. We are all people and not perfect." She admitted to him. He had smiled inwardly because she finally understood. Julia was no longer trying to control Joe or his kids. She was accepting.

She continued. "We are still communicating – peacefully, thankfully." Neither one of the couple had fought in two weeks. This was a step forward.

"Is he helping more and being more supportive of your relationship? Tell me what is happening?" The doc asked.

"He has been helping more around the house and with our finances. I am finding it easier to trust him. I have not gone through his phone in two months." This was a breakthrough of mammoth proportions for her. Trust – this was her down fall and the most important element of a relationship that she had to overcome.

They talked about everything that had occurred in her life since the end of last year – everything under the sun, except for the sun. The June day was luminous with it's magnificent blue sky, emerald green grass and trees, and the most important vitamin D source of all – the sun! It was glowing and radiant.

A perfect day for swimming. She thought.

The good doctor gave Julia some inter-personal skill advice. She was hopeful she would break out of her shell when it came to her self-esteem.

It was very early in the day. Her first vacation day in a month and Charlie's last day of school, and a half-day at that. His seventh grade year was coming to a close and it was time to celebrate. Not to mention later in the week was his thirteenth birthday as well.

She had vigorously planned the surprise pool party with her family, and Julia's cousin Mike was more than receptive to letting his pool be used at the highlight of the party. Julia was beyond excitement, and only needed to finish this morning's therapy session, before heading to get the cake, decorations, and food.

"Are you in there?" He had caught her drifting.

"Yes. Sorry." I have a lot on my mind with my son's birthday party tonight. She was embarrassed for being absent-minded in this moment.

"We can wrap this up early today. It is a beautiful day outside. I hope your son has a good birthday." He was genuine in his words. He wanted to get some extra work done and with the session ending early it gave him the time.

Chapter 15

Later that day Julia's tension was building. After a trip to the bakery to pick up Charlie's birthday cake followed by stop at the grocery store on the way out to her cousin's house. "Hi!" She walked up her cousin's driveway towards the open garage door carrying an abundance of filled bags with food and decorations. Two more trips to the vehicle later and the cake, gifts, and pool floaties were all process of being placed in their proper place.

I have one hour left. It all has to be in place. She thought anxiously as she whipped around the backyard in a blur of busyness. Her cousin Mike was still at work for another hour and a half and his wife Maura let Julia in, but had to leave to pick up her two children at school.

Her anxiousness turned into nervousness. Even though all the guests were close friends and family she had always been uneasy speaking in front of crowds and never liked any attention to be placed on her. There would be announcements. Luckily, her brother had a big mouth so she planned on recruiting him for the announcements.

The warm pool water was still and inviting. For being a June day it was hot outside, in the low eighties with no rain in the last few weeks. There was rarely a cloud in the sky and yet she picked at her thumbs, alternating left and right, not too much that people would notice; just enough to pacify her anxiety.

It was five pm and nearly all the guests had arrived. Julia's brother had brought Charlie.

"Oh wow! Thanks mom. A pool party!" Charlie hugged is mom and said hi to his friends and ran into the house to get changed into his swimsuit. No one had yet entered the pool and Julia, Maura, and Julia's mom were getting the food out of the house and setting the spread up outside. Most of the kids ran around doing various activities.

"When does Mike get done?" Julia asked Maura. She did not want the host to miss out on the festivities.

"He should be on his way." She replied happily. Mike, being a firefighter and EMT for a paid city fire department worked long multi-day shifts and spent an ample amount of time away from his family. "It's been two days…a forty-eight hour shift." She added admittedly missed her husband.

The party was nearly underway and as Julia, along with the other two women emerged from the kitchen through the sliding glass patio door there was yelling coming from the back yard.

"Oh God! No!" Where the first words Julia heard. She rushed with the others towards the rear of the yard, towards the pool located quite a ways from the house. The bright sunlight was blinding facing west in the later part of that hot summer day. A flood of screams, yelling, and confusion took over the perfectly decorated backyard and transformed the site to a state of eeriness.

"What's going on?" Julia stopped and was in a state of fast-paced confusion. The whole situation seemed unreal while

the older teenagers carried down the small person and laid the five year old girl on the ground next to the pool.

"Theresa!" Julia exasperated and fell to her knees instantly next to the young girl. Maura was hysterical that her youngest child lay unconscious on the ground and was turning blue. Everything happened so quickly in the next passing minutes, yet took a lifetime until help arrived. Mike was a short two minutes from his house when he got the phone call. He made it there in thirty seconds.

Why is this happening? I never should have had the party her. She would be ok. This is my fault. Julia performed CPR to the best of her ability and tried her best to concentrate on the counts and pressure of the chest depth while resuscitating. Though she had the CPR training she never had to use it – until now. Now, on her youngest and sweetest of family. She held back the tears. Most of the crowd could not hold back.

A million thoughts raced through Julia's mind seemingly instantly. Everything from Mike arriving, the paramedics, self-blame, Joseph and his kids, her family, among the worst of fears. She prayed and blew small amounts of air into the small lungs. The sirens were audible as were Mike's brakes on his truck as he pulled up and ran through his yard. He had to save her. If anyone could save her it would be him.

"Mike!" Maura cried and screamed sitting on the ground in shambles. Her brother and sister trying to keep her in control the best they could. Julia moved over to have Mike take her place above Theresa. He glared at Julia before resuming compressions.

This is my fault. She instantly blamed herself and the effects of the Prozac could not be found.

The first responders, ambulance, and paramedic unit arrived nearly all together. So much for the first responders. "Back here!" Several family members had rapidly escorted the emergency crews into the backyard and were getting all the info. Five-year old girl in the pool alone for approximately three to four minutes; the group of teens found her upon them entering the pool and fished her out. 911 was then called.

Text book. Julia thought. She didn't speak much and waited for the blame of the party in the first place. In truth, Julia took full responsibility in her mind. She held everything together quite well now, but give it an hour when she was by herself. She would do her best not to hate herself for this.

Everyone prayed and cried and tried to remain positive while the ambulance pulled away with lights and sirens going. The hospital was only one and a half miles away and she was alive. Unconscious still, but alive. Julia hugged Charlie and missed Joseph. She wanted him here with her more than anything. Joseph was two counties over with his family. His grandfather was given one week to live by the doctor and Hospice was there. The pool party had been planned for months and she felt bad that she was not there with Joe to be supportive.

"You gonna call Joe?" Charlie asked his mom.

"Not yet. Him and his family are going through a lot also. I don't want to bother him." She somberly said and hugged her son tighter.

Chapter 16

"Hello?" Julia answered the phone sitting on her love seat. She knew it was her mom from the caller ID and she was waiting for news on Theresa. Julia had been praying all night and it was ten o'clock.

"She's doing much better. Maura just called me a few minutes ago. I'm calling most of the family to let them know." Her mom informed her. "She's out of the ER and on the second floor in a room. They are going to keep her over night for observation."

She listened to her mother go on about the details and did her best to ignore the booming thunder approaching from the west. The day was hot and storms formed over the lake and were slowly making their way on land.

"Oh thank God." Julia was relieved. Charlie had stayed over his friend Roger's house. They went to go see the new Spiderman movie and did what teenagers do while Julia did what she did best – worry. Joseph was still with his family and called her an hour ago. His grandfather had passed away quietly surrounded by his entire family. Joe's kids were with him and their family and were understandable upset by the entire situation.

Julia reluctantly told Joe about Theresa's incident in the pool. She did want to downplay his hardship, but rather needed someone to talk to. She still blamed herself for Theresa's accident. Joe understood and wanted to be there for her.

"I'm sorry hun, glad she is ok." He reassured her over the phone. She listened through more claps of thunder and sobbed.

"It's my fault. If I didn't have the party there this wouldn't have happened." There were no storms where he was fifty miles away from home. He had no problem hearing her. He knew she was beating up herself inside.

"Julia. Stop. You didn't do anything. It was *her* house and your cousins should know to watch her and the other kids around the pool. *They* just assumed that so many people were there that someone else was watching her. Maura should have been watching Theresa, not you." He was right and she felt better by his reassurance. Even in his moment of deep loss he was there for her, relentlessly. She was thankful for him being in her life.

"Thank you Joe. I love you so much. I am so sorry about your grandfather. Please pass my condolences on to your mom and the rest of your family. I will talk to you later hun."

"I love you more." He not only said it, but he meant it. She hung up the phone and walked around the house closing all of the windows to keep out the fastly falling stinging rain and wind.

The End...

After months of therapy and working hard in all aspects of her personal life she felt like she was ahead. Julia had a positive attitude, weight loss goals being met, a new promotion, and a happy relationship. It was a holiday, our country was celebrating and she was going to celebrate. The Fourth of July was here. Though June had proved to be a month of mixed weather with floods at times and bone-dry at others the conditions were finally smoothing out in the present forecast.

"Hi mom. I'm leaving the store and we are on our way." Julia, Joseph, and the kids all piled into the vehicle and drove to the nearby state park. The family had reserved a pavilion along the shore-line of Lake Erie. The half a century year old pavilions were a continuous part of Julia's family holidays.

"Are we there yet?" JJ asked. Sitting bored to no end in the middle of the two older kids.

"Yes." Joseph said as while pulling into the parking lot. The ride was only a few miles to the entrance of the park and an additional two miles to this particular spot. There were no clearly defined parking spots in the dirt lots of the park, just lots of rocks sitting above dirt.

"Everyone needs to help and grab a bag." She directed the comment to the three children in the back seat. The July heat and mid afternoon warmth shown bright through the vehicle windows with an unavoidable blindness. They parked next to Julia's mom's black Honda Civic. The dust from the parking lot left a fresh dirty layer on the vehicle.

"Hi grandma!" Charlie was first out of the car. He yelled and gave her a hug. Julia's father was already in route carrying a large blue Coleman cooler to the pavilion.

"Hi Charlie." She hugged her grandson. "Can you carry this for me?" She piled blue and white food containers in his arms and bags in his hands. Julia's entire mother's side of the family was going to be there at the picnic just as all the previous picnics through all the years.

Julia's mom had several brothers and sisters with kids and grandkids of their own. They were quite the large group. The brood all treaded through the sand up the hill towards the tables and pavilion. Most of the family was already there including her brother and the most precious of guests, Theresa - excited, full of life, and past her near death experience. Mike and Maura equally celebrated and didn't give undesirable thoughts a chance to manifest in conversation; it was a day to celebrate.

It's a good day.

Everyone brought a dish and chipped in for the hamburgers and hot dogs. The uncles grilled the food and the women chatted and set everything up while the kids all ran around and played in the sand. The wind cooperated though clouds were slowly rolling in. All of Julia's cousins stayed to eat and a few had left as the day came to a close.

She had no radical emotions that day, just happiness. Which was a rarity. No fights, no unrealized paranoia, just a normal day. It was better than a normal day – It was July 4th!

"When it's dark were doing fireworks!" One of the uncles bellowed and all the kids met his enthusiasm in reply. Multiple "Ya!'s and cheers" came from the crowd of youngsters.

Twilight came and anticipation grew. Julia and her mom and aunt got the fireworks ready. Theresa, in celebration ran along the shoreline. A faint shouting of "I'm free!" was heard. The clouds filled the sky and the last glimpse of light shimmered on the lake water giving the appearance of gray to all around. Not bright, not dark, just gray.

Julia sat on the bench snuggled up with Joe, his arm around her back and just watched. She felt free, like the younger child running briskly along the shore line. The dark waves nearly matching the gray encompassed sky gave way to the heat of the impending summer night. The weather was perfect.

Yes, it was a good day.

Author Biography

This is my second book. As a writer I wanted to share my personal experiences with codependency. Of course, all the names and places have been changed.

I have found the paramount author Melody Beattie has written several books on codependency. With the exception of a few authors, there is not a large volume of texts devoted to this issue. As an author I hope to reach people on a personal level who have had the same type of experiences and diagnosis of codependency.

With the help of my therapist and support from my family I try my best to succeed in everyday life with these challenges. I wish success to all codependents out there. There will be sunny days and cloudy days, but never give up and thank you for reading!

Presque Isle State Park at Twilight
Erie, PA

References:

Beattie, Melody. <u>Codependent No More: How to Stop Controlling Others and Start Caring for Yourself</u>. Center City: Hazelden, 1992.

Beattie, Melody. <u>The New Codependency: Help and Guidence for Today's Generation</u>. New York: Simon, 2009.